MODELLING WWII SOFT-SKINNED MILITARY VEHICLES

Osprey Modelling Manuals
Volume 11

Rodrigo Hernández Cabos

OSPREY

Osprey Modelling Manuals 11

MODELLING WWII SOFT-SKINNED MILITARY VEHICLES

First published in Great Britain in 2000 by Osprey Publishing, Elms Court, Chapel Way, Botley, Oxford OX2 9LP, United Kingdom.
Email: info@ospreypublishing.com

© Accion Press, S. A., C/Ezequiel Solana, 16, 28017, Madrid, Spain. Euromodelismo. Depósito Legal M-19729-1992

ISBN 1 84176 139 7

English edition packaged by Compendium, 1st Floor, 43 Frith Street, London, W1V 5TE

00 01 02 03 04   10 9 8 7 6 5 4 3 2 1

Publication Manager: Rodrigo Hernández Cabos
Photographs: Salvador Gómez Mico, Rodrigo Hernández Cabos
Modelling Team: Carlos de Diego Vaquerizo, David Romero Utrero, Critóbal Vergara Durán, Aurelio Gimeno Ruiz, Joaquin García Gazquez, Angel Iñigo Hernández, Manuel Rodríguez Aguilar, Miguel Jimenez Martín, Jorge López Terrer, Jesús Huélamo Pérez

Printed in Spain

For a catalogue of all books published by Osprey Military and Aviation please contact:

The Marketing Manager, Osprey Direct UK, PO Box 140, Wellingborough, Northants, NN8 4ZA, United Kingdom. Tel. (0)1933 443863, Fax (0)1933 443849.
Email: info@ospreydirect.co.uk

The Marketing Manager, Osprey Direct USA, PO Box 130, Sterling Heights, MI 48311-0130, USA. Tel. 248 394 6191, Fax 248 394 6194. Email: info@ospreydirectusa.com

Visit Osprey at:
www.ospreypublishing.com

INTRODUCTION

While tanks and armoured cars have the edge for excitement, there's no doubting the fact that soft-skinned military vehicles are essential for most dioramas. The trouble is that they tend to be more difficult to model than a tank; they tend to have lots of bits of kit — personal weapons and clothing, complicated awnings and windshields — and, often, a number of figures, too. It is important, therefore to be able to model them well — and that is what the eleventh of Osprey's Modelling Manuals comes in. It provides expert advice, professional tips and pointers, and detailed technical knowledge to help with model-making, scratch-building, superdetailing and, in particular, painting these tricky vehicles.

What an intriguing mixture of vehicles can be found inside. First up is the classic German Schwimmwagen, the amphibious vehicle used for command and reconaissance duties all over the battlefields of WWII; then there's the German half-track artillery tractor, the SdKf. 11 and the armoured half-track SdKfz 7/1 with its anti-aircraft installation; it is followed by the GAZ-67B — the Russian jeep; then we move to the desert war and a desert-camouflaged Bedford MW; next is an end of the war cavalcade protecting a Dodge WC-56 3/4-ton jeep with a VIP passenger — General George Patton; after this northern German interlude we move to desert encampment and an SAS jeep, its bearded crew armed to the teeth with a variety of weapons; then there is the remarkable BM-13 Katyusha multiple rocke launcher — the famous 'Stalin's Organ'; an RAF Albion AM463 fuel bowser; a Dodge WC-54 ambulance; the VW-86 Kübelwagen; and finally a Willys Jeep.

Who can say that soft-skinned vehicles are not interesting?

KFZ 1/20 SCHWIMMWAGEN

Starting in the 1930s, the German army experimented with several designs for amphibious vehicles, amongst which the Trippel was the best.

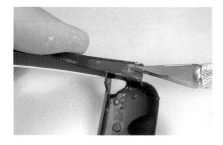

Using a small drill, hollow out the areas corresponding to the ventilation grille.

In Germany in 1940 the Schwimmwagen, Model 128, appeared; it was designed by Ferdinand Porsche and 150 were manufactured. Two years later the production of Model 166 began. This vehicle had smaller dimensions than the previous Schwimmwagen and stayed in production until 1944, by which time a massive 14,500 units had been made. This amphibious vehicle, with 4 x 4 traction, had the appearance of a boat even

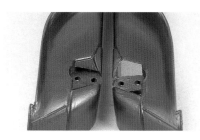

Use a blade to reduce the thickness of the fender.

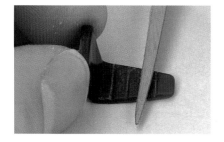

In the front end, hollow out the areas through which the transmission-steering bars go.

Using a file, engrave the pleat found on the back of the seat.

Various elements belonging to the boat interior.

The completed chassis together with the seats.

The tiny belts which hold the propeller system in place.

being equipped with a rear propeller. On lowering, the propeller automatically received power from the engine and could produce a speed of 6 knots when in water.

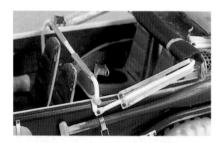

These special wheels are made of resin and sold by ADV.

Plastic and etched-brass details are added to the propeller system.

The rods of the convertible roof are made from etched-brass strips and plastic rods.

General view of all the elements which make up the interior.

The exhausts, rods and bonnet fastenings were custom made.

The pieces in front of the exhaust silencer serve to hold a tripod.

The 1,131cc 4-cylinder air-cooled engine could run at 3,300rpm. This allowed the vehicle to reach speeds of up to 80km/h on land and gave it an operational range of 520km, using up approximately 9 litres of fuel every 100km. The vehicle weighed 910kg, and could hold a total of up to 1,345kg. With five front gears and one back gear, the Volkswagen Schwimmwagen Model 166 was 3.825m long, 1.480m wide and 1.615m high. The distance between axles was 2m with a distance to the ground surface of 0.24m.

Widely used by the German Army on the Eastern Front and then eventually throughout

This canvas not only adds another interesting element to the model, but usefully hides a flaw in the tyre.

The canvas is painted with brown and dark green camouflage markings.

many details have to be custom made — etched-brass replacements (we used ones from Eduard) only solved the most basic problems.

We started by gluing together the two parts of the body. Subsequently we hollowed out the area where the ventilation grille needs to fit and used a blade to refine the rear side bumper.

We also needed to open gaps

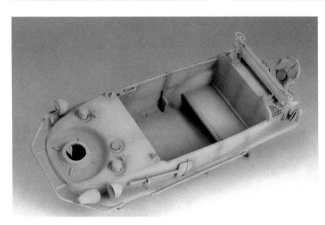

The vehicle early in the painting stage with the base colour and the first additional tones painted over the surface.

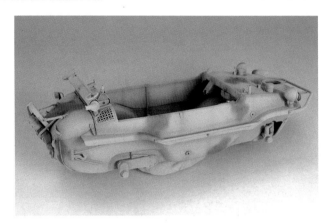

The green camouflage markings should be applied erratically but well apart.

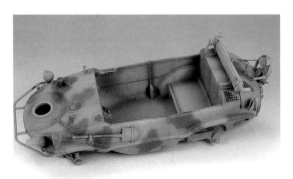

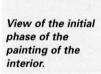

In the empty areas apply brown markings.

View of the initial phase of the painting of the interior.

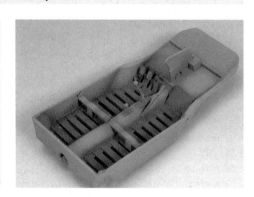

Europe, this vehicle always delivered excellent results in joint and reconnaissance missions because of its unique ability to overcome natural obstacles and cross bodies of water in places where other vehicles could not follow.

Assembly

This Italeri model (scale ½0) has been on the market for many years, something that becomes obvious upon closer inspection when it can be seen that many details are missing. Therefore

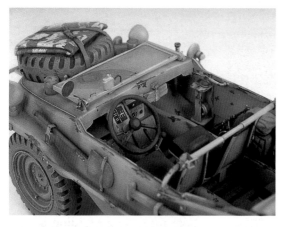

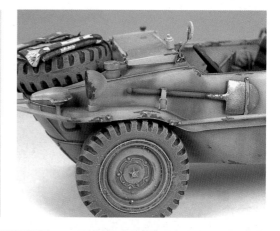

A detailed view of the elaborate interior paint job.

Scraped paint on the front of the vehicle.

A satin varnish was applied to the oar.

Colour Table

Tamiya (acrylics)
Black (XF-1)
Matt aluminum (XF-16)
Earth (XF-52)
Cinnamon (XF-52)
Olive green (XF-58)
Dark yellow (XF-60)
Brownish red (XF-64)

Marabú (varnish)
Mattlack

Humbrol (enamel)
Oak (71)

Titan (oils)
White 4
Burnt earth umber (78)
Yellow ochre (88)
Transparent gold ochre (94)
Burnt earth sienna (96)

This shows the gradation of colours, with the lighter shades at the top.

in the front end of the vehicle so the steering bars could go through. The joints of the various parts that make up the bodywork were imitated with strands of stretched plastic thread.

We built the bumpers and side handles from Evergreen rods; other details were improved by using sheets of plastic of varying degrees of thickness.

In the interior, the bow end of the boat was elongated with plastic sheet. Etched-brass handles and other small custom-made pieces were also added.

The metal machine gun body, the munitions drums, and the small compartment next to the dashboard also needed building.

Returning to the exterior, we needed to build the bonnet clasps, and then add details to the actual propeller, which is presented in a fairly basic way in the kit. We then added etched-brass pieces and belts made from copper strands and strips of tin to hold the propeller.

The original kit exhaust pipe was discarded and a new one was built along with an enclosure to lower the propeller. We also had to make the pieces that hold the tripod behind the exhaust pipe, using elements of

The convertible roof and seats were painted using an airbrush.

The interior was completed by adding a variety of equipment and accessories.

After finishing the vehicle, place the model in a suitable environment.

The basic figure is from Hornet but the head was changed and the equipment added.

The fountain is made from a combination of plaster, putty and plastic strips.

Materials

Schwimmwagen, Italeri ½₀:
  Ref. 310
Wheels are ADV Azimut:
  Ref. 35318
Etched-brass pieces from
  Eduard: Ref. 35.008

plastic and etched-brass material. The convertible roof was completely remodelled, including the skeleton rods.

We finished by adding some pieces from a Hasegawa Kübel kit, including a shovel, headlight coverings, and the windscreen wiper. The wide, all-terrain wheels were from an ADV Azimut kit.

Painting

We started by adding a base mix of dark yellow and cinnamon, to which yellow and earth were added as required. The camouflage was made up of irregular blotches of an olive green and brown-red colour mixed with a small amount of dark yellow. After painting the model was left to dry for several days before having general washes of brown and ochre applied.

To finish, we outlined all the edges and details using a darker tone. Then oak-coloured enamel highlights were applied with a dry brush.

To simulate chipping and wear, we used a mix of black and reddish-brown acrylics which were lightened by applying a burnt sienna wash, plus metallic touches wherever we thought them necessary. General dirt and grime effects and the varnishing were done in the usual way.

For the camouflage outfit over the spare tyre we used Vallejo acrylics, and a technique of successively applying lighter coats; the base is a mix of pastel green and white, while the camouflage tones were made up from chocolate brown, olive green and military green.

7

SdKfz 11

After their successes with tracked vehicles built and operated during World War I — such as the Marienwagen and the Krapfprotze — the German High Command instructed engineering companies to continue to develop tracked vehicles for battlefield operations.

The artillery and other branches of the armed forces required a tractor-type vehicle in order to tow heavy equipment to and from the battlefield. This vehicle needed to be fast and capable of operating in a variety of terrain. In 1932, contracts were signed with six different German companies to develop more vehicles of this kind; they were to be varied in size and classified according to weight. One such contract was signed with Hansa-Lloid-Goliath AG of Bremen to build a 3-ton tractor.

The first prototype of this series, designated HLKI 2, was built in 1934, and the improved versions HLKI 3 and 4 came out two years later. In 1937 the

HLKI 5 was built. Like its predecessors, it had a 6-cylinder, Borgward L-3500L engine. The final version, the HLKI 6, was built in 1939, and was equipped

with a Maybach HL-38 motor — later replaced by the HL-42.

Officially called *Leichte Zugkraftwagen 3t (SdKfz 11) typ k1 6*, this vehicle was kept in

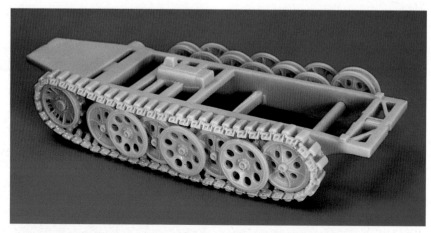

General view of the chassis, track and wheels. The track is wrapped around the wheels after gently warming them with a hair dryer to make them pliable.

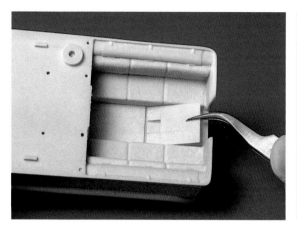

The towing hook was made using part of the original piece plus plastic and tin.

The nonslip plate was cut to size from a resin sheet, although various etched-brass pieces could also have been used.

production until 1944, by which time a total of 8,800 had been built. There were six versions, each for different tasks; primarily they were used as artillery tractors, towing 105mm guns; they also served as rocket launcher platforms and for transporting munitions. In yet another role they were also used to tow the 75 and 88mm anti-tank guns.

The chassis served as the basis on which the SdKfz 251 armoured infantry vehicle was built — this had 23 versions, and a production run of some 15,000 units.

When fully loaded, the SdKfz 11 weighed 7,200kg and carried a crew of eight. With a length of 5.55m, a width of 2m and a height of 2.15m, its operational range could be up to 275km, reaching a maximum speed of 52.5km/h. The petrol motor was a 6-cylinder, 100cv HL-42 TUKRM. The Hanomag transmission was 4 x 2 forward and 1 x 2 back. The tank capacity was 110 litres, and the width of the track 280mm.

Assembly

We used a $\frac{1}{35}$ scale kit from the French manufacturer Al-By. After cleaning up any pieces with small imperfections, we began with the assembly of the chassis, tracks and wheels. The tracks were heated with a hair dryer and then quickly wrapped around the wheels. The towing hook was painted with a tin and

plastic rod. For the inside, we sanded down the seats in order to smooth out the bumpy surface texture. Then we cut new nonslip plates to size from resin and attached them to the deck of the vehicle. We used etched-brass plates made by Scale Link — these are intended to be used as moulds from which copies can be made.

Above the back seats, we had to remodel the bodywork with pieces cut from a 0.20mm thick aluminium sheet, measuring 9 x 39mm. These were then curved by pressing them around a

paintbrush handle. Finally, we used plastic to add details to the cabin including new instruments on the dashboard.

Once the inside was complete, the outside was ready to be worked on. After removing the ugly side details, we made new doors for the munitions storage area from a 0.13mm thick plastic sheet, as well as the corresponding plastic rivets. We then placed a series of small hooks on the hood, (from the etched-brass pieces intended for the Puma).

Behind each front wing we

The aluminium pieces are curved using a brush handle and a metal ruler.

After gluing the two pieces, details are added to the inside of the back entrance with plastic strips and rivets.

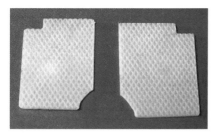

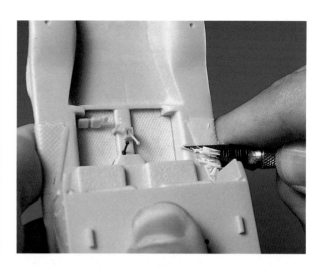

marked a joint with the scriber and added a total of six plastic ribs (three on each side). A Notek (obtained from any plastic model) was placed over the left bumper. The last job here was to rebuild the railing belonging to the convertible

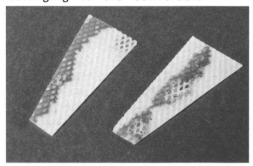

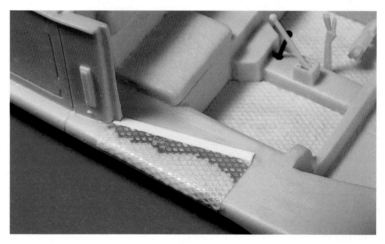

These are the new foot rests re-cut to size.

After gluing these pieces, the ends can be curved by gently heating them with a hair dryer.

The cabin deck was entirely rebuilt and new details were added.

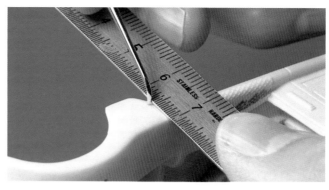

A joint is marked on each side with a scriber

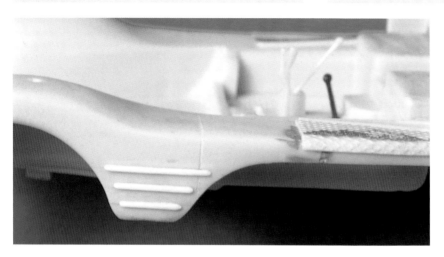

The ribs are made using strips of plastic.

using a dry brush, then washing softly with different tones.

To paint the outside, we masked off the already painted areas in order to not spoil them. A dark yellow base was laid down before starting on the camouflage. The camouflage pattern was created by painting small zigzags, which never entirely covered the base tone. To obtain the red-brown, we mixed 65% matt brown, 30%

These new doors for the munitions compartment were made from a plastic sheet, 0.13mm thick.

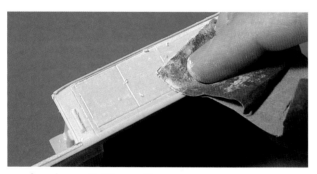

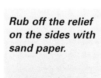

Rub off the relief on the sides with sand paper.

Details added to the doors include tin and steel strips, and a photo-engraved lock.

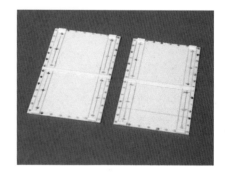

roof, using a 0.64mm Evergreen rod.

Painting

We began with the inside where, after applying a dark yellow base and lightening with white, the non-slip plates were washed with beige brown, black, leather red and burnt umber acrylics. After applying base colour black to the seats, we gave them a worn-out look by airbrushing a mix of earth brown and white. We finished painting the interior by applying dirt and shading

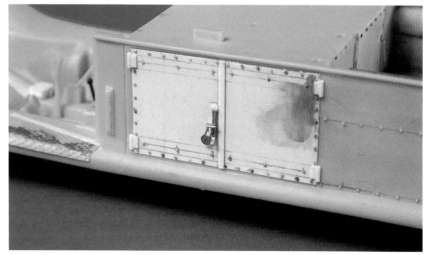

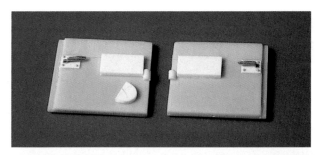

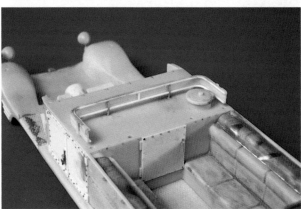

dark yellow and 5% red; for the green, we combined 75% olive green with 15% dark yellow and 15% khaki.

After painting all of the markings, and only using red brown, we airbrushed out some small spots in the yellow spaces, thus allowing brown to dominate the colour scheme.

Subsequently we added the effects of dirt, deterioration, etc.

For the dry-brush work, a cream-coloured enamel was applied. The only thing left to mention is that the chains were painted by

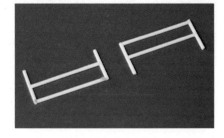

The top handrails were made using 0.64mm rods.

applying a successive series of washes, combining leather red, black and burnt umber acrylics.

The rubber brake shoes and the tyres were painted by combining black and khaki brown; afterwards this piece was dry brushed with khaki brown and dark sand.

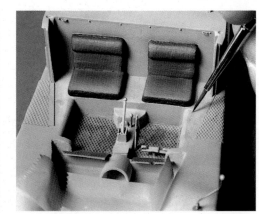

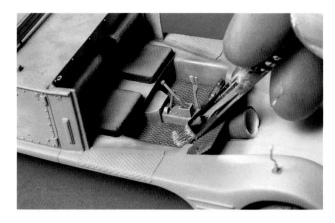

After applying several light washes to the anti-slip surface, the effect of polished metal can be replicated by using a dry brush and a mix of steel grey and silver.

Highlights on the worn seats were airbrushed using a mix of white and an earth tone.

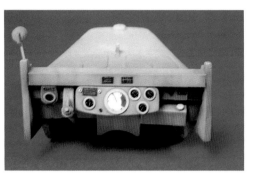

The dashboard was painted with a brush, and the glass-covered instruments were rendered using a bright acrylic varnish.

Once the interior is well masked, the dark yellow base colour is applied to the vehicle.

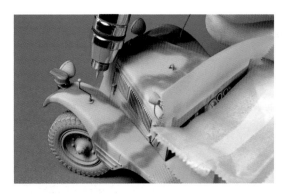

First, the brown markings are painted, each one of which is made up of fine, cross-hatched lines, which never entirely cover the base colour.

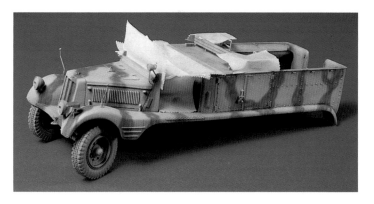

Leave large gaps between the markings, allowing enough space for the last colour.

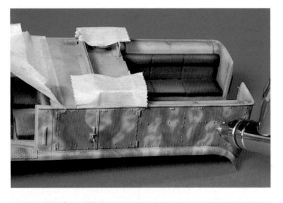

Add very small red-brown spots in the empty main body colour.

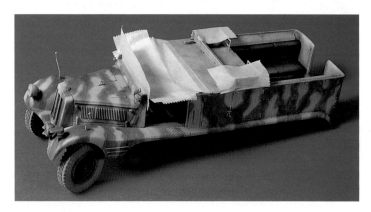

The vehicle after the green markings were added.

Masks can be used to paint the 2nd Panzer Division trident — but it is easier to paint this item in separate parts.

The look of the vehicle has changed, with brown now being the predominant colour.

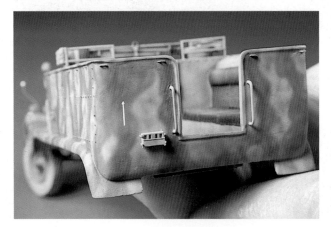

Start of the central painting stage.

The horizontal bar is added later .

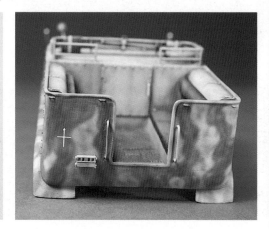

The sides are painted next.

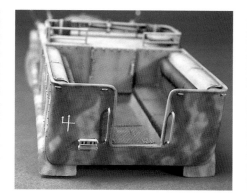

The completed trident tactical sign. If painting is not your strength, this symbol is sold on transfer sheets.

Using 0.2mm acetate, the area covered by the windscreen wiper is masked off.

This is the resulting effect after airbrushing on desert yellow and removing the masks.

Before assembling the chassis, it is important to paint the tracks and wheels.

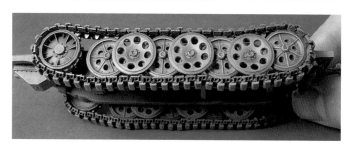

COLOUR TABLE

Tamiya acrylics
Matt black (XF-1)
Matt white (XF-2)
Matt red (XF-7)
Matt brown (XF-10)
Khaki (XF-49)
Olive green (XF-56)
Desert yellow (XF-59)
Dark yellow (XF-60)

Vallejo acrylics
Leather red (818)
Dark sand (847)
Beige brown (875)
Burnt umber (941)
Matt black (950)
Khaki brown (988)

Oil colours
Natural sienna
Titan white
Burnt umber
English red
Dark cobalt blue
Green

Humbrol enamels
Matt white (34)
Matt cream (103)

Tamiya enamels
Steel grey (X-10)
Silver (X-11)

Varnishes
Marabú Mattlack
Model Colour
bright varnish

SdKfz 7/1
Self-propelled anti-aircraft guns

This kit is excellent, if expensive, but still needs extras and details poached from other models in order to make it look more realistic. The final result was extremely satisfying after an interesting challenge.

After checking out the etched-brass from Show Modelling, we quickly realised that there was a lack of detail in the model; for example, the hood closure and rifle supports were not included. Also, for this vehicle we needed another addition — namely the tyres — which we found in the kit Bussing 4500 from Azimut.

History

In 1928, the German firm Krauss-Maffei had the idea of designing and building a series of agricultural tractors. However, four years passed before Dr. Ing Mayor Nehring, director of the

Detail of the finished vehicle showing the etched-brass side grille, the specially narrowed doors and the welding spots emphasised.

Rings were added to the front plates and the deposit case was left open.

Cabling and electric gadgetry was added to the quadruple canon plus other details to the viewing device (sights?).

national tractors programme, drew up the criteria for a design contest for a new type of tracked vehicle. The requirements were to optimise tracked technical characteristics, at the same time advancing the technology of such machines. In Lennep in March 1933 the winner was announced as Krauss-Maffei.

Thanks to the firm's influential connections, Krauss-Maffei had won the contest at the expense of the Bussing-Nag proposal. By this time, Hitler was already in power and prioritising military industry; several projects, such as the Krauss-Maffei were put into action immediately. The

The viewing device is new and was made using the elements attached to the single 20mm canon piece from Tamiya.

initial order was for 80 vehicles, 30 of which were sent to Spain, where their unquestionable quality and excellent service were demonstrated on the battlefield. As a consequence, they won the gold medal in the industrial fair celebrated in Berlin in 1937.

When World War II began, 100 of these tractors were already in use, and by the end of the war this number had risen to over 12,000, and it is probably true to say that these vehicles saw action on all fronts.

In 1940, studies were made to modify the tractor into a weapon-bearing, anti-aircraft vehicle. The series started with the Flak 38 and finished with the 3.7cm Flak 36. One conversion that failed was the attempt to carry a 5cm weapon; weight problems prevented the development going beyond the second prototype stage.

After 1943 variants with armoured cabins began to be produced. In 1944, versions equipped with the 3.7cm Flak appeared offered by Puchala

and NKC. Variants of this vehicle exist in model form, with changes found in the armoured cabin, rails and sides. Many of these modifications are only sketchy (as in the Tamiya kit), while others are complete — as we show here.

Assembly

The most detailed work on this model is the motor, which is entirely customised. This

In this bird's eye view of the vehicle, the cab hatchways, the tarpaulin, and details along the rear side are visible.

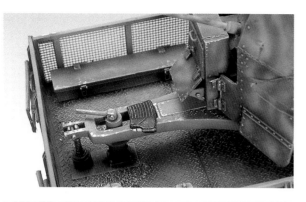

The adjustments made to the base of the weapon involve new tubes and rods from Evergreen.

The door of the right side compartment is reworked to be left open.

By replacing the original tracks for new ones from Model Kasten, the look of the vehicle changes.

some basic mechanical knowledge (as well as basing the work on similar vehicles), successful execution of this part of the job is not too difficult.

Painting

This vehicle is to be painted by combining dark yellow (Tamiya XF-60), a drop of yellow (10%)

The effects of scuffing and wear that appear in the most used and stepped on parts of the vehicle are made with metallic grey, finely applied with the tip of a brush; a light and diluted touch of rust, dark brown and orange have also been applied.

and a bit of white (15%). Some olive green and red-brown are mixed with the yellow (10%), in order to obtain a better colour.

Before painting the chassis and caterpillar tracks, cover these elements with a coat of fine sand mixed with putty. Initially, apply a black matt, then after painting, finish the job with a dry brush and ink.

Reference Books

Die Halbkettenfahrzeuge des deutschen Heeres 1909-1945. Motorbuch Verlag

Military Modelling, December 1981

Wheels & Tracks, No 12

D-Day to Berlin, Arms and Armour Press

Die Leichte und Mittlere Flak 1906-1945, Podzum-Pallas

happily gave us the opportunity to remove the sides of the motor compartment altogether — a common feature for vehicles operating in warm climates.

Predictably, clear photographic reference is not easily available. Although this engine has been well documented in the Motorbuch Verlag book on German tractors, the specific elements that surround this particular section are not clearly shown. Nevertheless, by paying close attention to the photographs and possessing

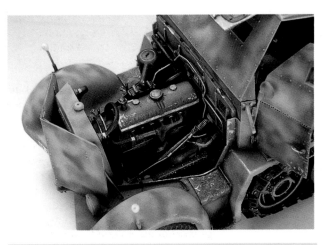

The motor is one of the most important features. It is made using a variety of custom-built pieces.

The engine cable system should be put together as carefully and realistically as possible.

The original tyres were replaced by ones belonging to the Bussing 4500 made by Azimut.

COLOUR CHART

Tamiya acrilycs

Base colour	Dark Yellow (XF-60)
1st camouflage	Olive Green (XF-58)
2nd camouflage	Red Brown (XF-64)

Interior

Base colour	Dark Yellow (XF-60)
Tracks	Hull Red (XF-9)
Colour wash	Matt black (XF-1)
Dry brush	Metallic grey
	Olive green (XF-56)

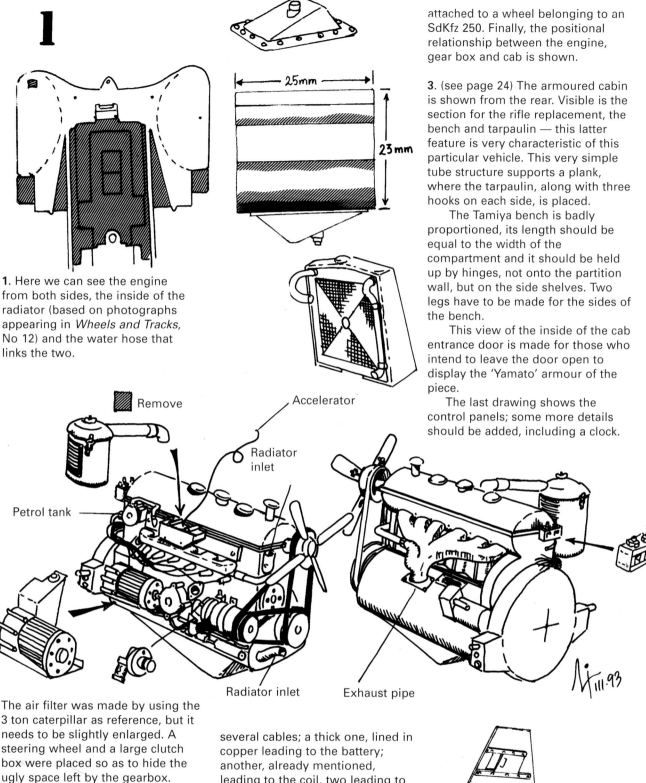

1

1. Here we can see the engine from both sides, the inside of the radiator (based on photographs appearing in *Wheels and Tracks*, No 12) and the water hose that links the two.

Remove

Accelerator

Radiator inlet

Petrol tank

Radiator inlet

Exhaust pipe

The air filter was made by using the 3 ton caterpillar as reference, but it needs to be slightly enlarged. A steering wheel and a large clutch box were placed so as to hide the ugly space left by the gearbox.

2. (see page 24) Three drawings of the engine and engine compartment. The first shows the space before the engine is put into place. In particular note the coil with its three cables — the right, the left connecting to the battery (passing through the fuse box) and the central cable leading to the distributor. The fuse box includes several cables; a thick one, lined in copper leading to the battery; another, already mentioned, leading to the coil, two leading to the control panel, one connecting to the horn, and finally, three connecting to the rear lights and the headlights.

Three cables come from the pedals: the central leads to the accelerator, another to the left clutch and a third, divided in two, leads to the track brakes.

The steering consists of a bar

attached to a wheel belonging to an SdKfz 250. Finally, the positional relationship between the engine, gear box and cab is shown.

3. (see page 24) The armoured cabin is shown from the rear. Visible is the section for the rifle replacement, the bench and tarpaulin — this latter feature is very characteristic of this particular vehicle. This very simple tube structure supports a plank, where the tarpaulin, along with three hooks on each side, is placed.

The Tamiya bench is badly proportioned, its length should be equal to the width of the compartment and it should be held up by hinges, not onto the partition wall, but on the side shelves. Two legs have to be made for the sides of the bench.

This view of the inside of the cab entrance door is made for those who intend to leave the door open to display the 'Yamato' armour of the piece.

The last drawing shows the control panels; some more details should be added, including a clock.

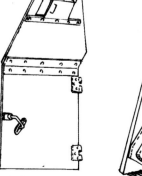

4. View of the back of the box showing the steps, how the bolts should look — made from infantry trench shovels — the back end of the chassis and the way that the compartment doors close.

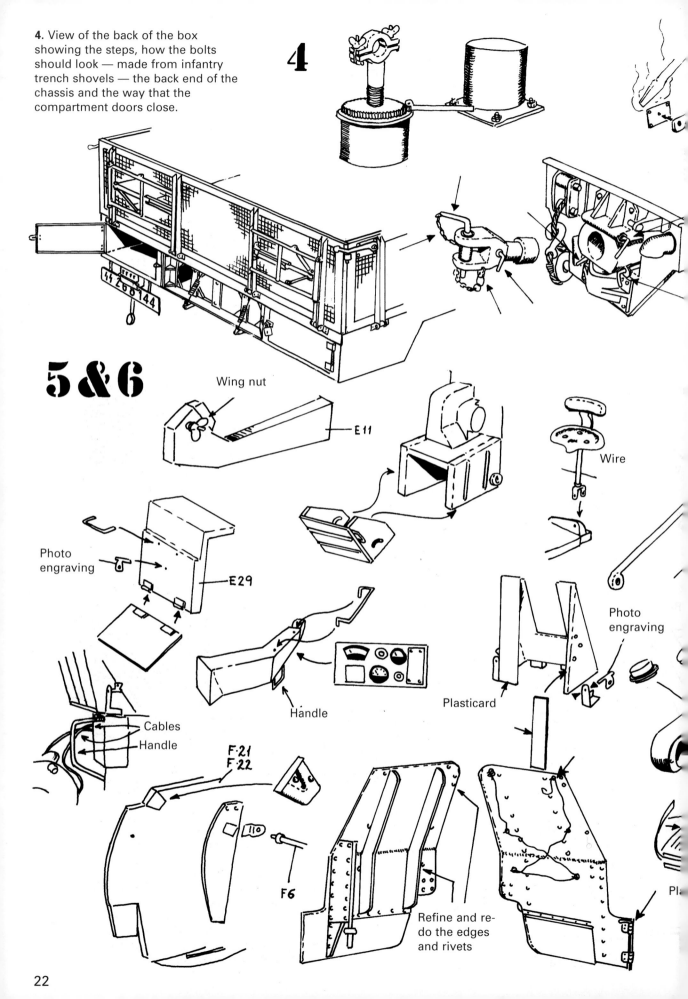

4

5 & 6

Wing nut

E 11

Wire

Photo engraving

E29

Photo engraving

Plasticard

Handle

Cables

Handle

F·21
F·22

F6

Refine and re-do the edges and rivets

7. This drawing shows off the intricacies of the armour, the actual shape of the viewing device and the details of the munitions compartment.

7

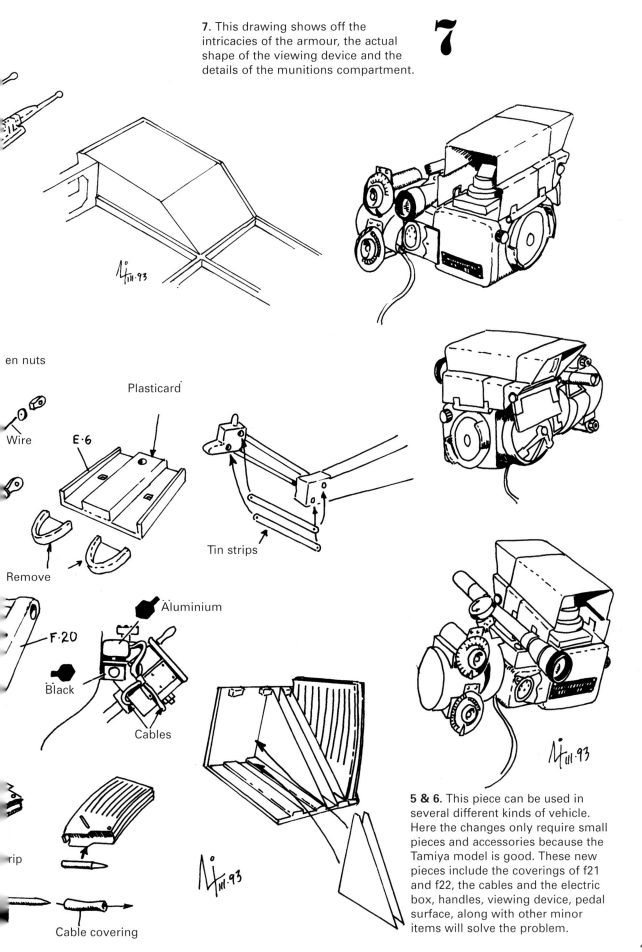

en nuts

Plasticard

Wire

E·6

Remove

Tin strips

Aluminium

F·20

Black

Cables

rip

Cable covering

5 & 6. This piece can be used in several different kinds of vehicle. Here the changes only require small pieces and accessories because the Tamiya model is good. These new pieces include the coverings of f21 and f22, the cables and the electric box, handles, viewing device, pedal surface, along with other minor items will solve the problem.

2

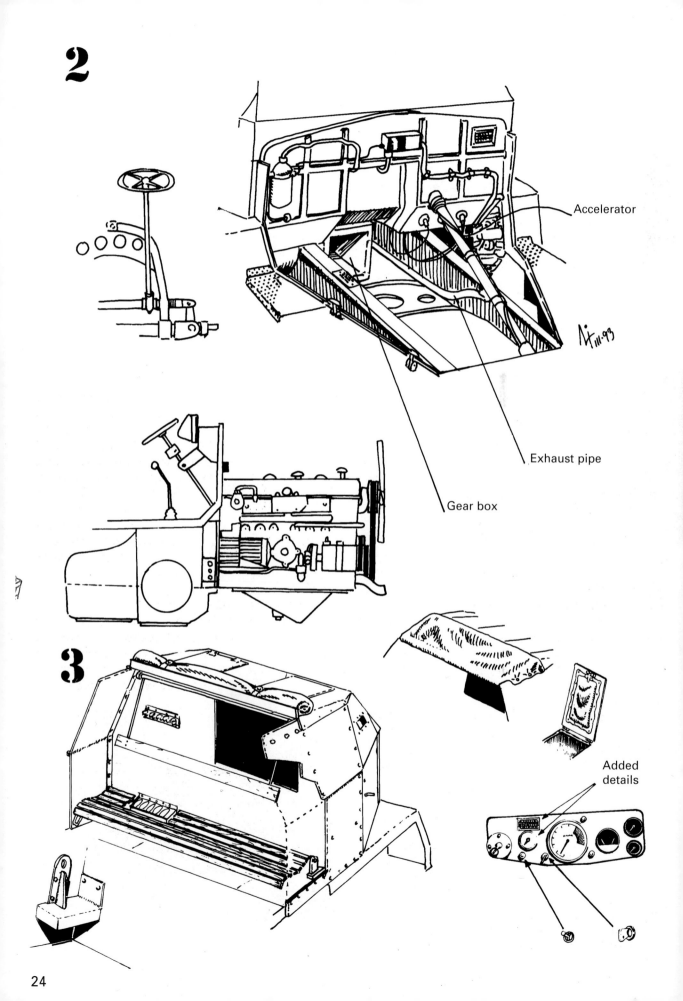

Accelerator

Exhaust pipe

Gear box

3

Added details

GAZ-67B

In the USSR, during 1943, a new all-terrain vehicle was developed called the GAZ-67.

I nspired by the Willys Jeep MB, the Gorkovski Avtomobiliny Zadov technicians set out to build their own all-terrain vehicle. Taking the BA-20, they kept the same motor, but shortened the chassis around which they designed a simple new body. The result was designated the GAZ-67. It was further modified by elongating the chassis by 22cm and redesignated GAZ-67A.

During summer 1943 the GAZ-67B appeared — the only difference from the previous version was the shape of the radiator grille, a petrol tank placed below the back seat and an indicator on the dashboard. Another version, the GAZ-46MAV, was amphibious.

The GAZ-67B first saw action at Kursk, where it proved robust and fast over all kinds of terrain in its role as a light artillery tractor and reconnaissance vehicle. The GAZ-67B was manufactured until 1953 and distributed to many Eastern Bloc countries. The design of the armoured BA-64B was based on this vehicle.

Specification

The GAZ-67B was 3.35m long, 1.685m wide and 1.7m tall. The vehicle ran on a 4-cylinder, 3.285cc GAZ-MM water-cooled engine, providing 54cv and 2,800rpm. The transmission was 4 x 4. The vehicle could reach maximum speeds of 90km/h, and could run 500km without a fuel refill. It weighed 1,320kg and could carry up to four people or 325kg of weight.

Assembly

This French kit from Al-By is of the highest quality. It is made up of 11 pieces and its assembly is so simple that no instructions are included with the model!

The numbers and letters on the license plates were done freehand using an 0.2 pen over an adhesive sheet.

A combination of airbrush and regular brushwork was used to paint the vehicle. Before starting, make sure that the brush tip is absolutely perfect in order to paint the very smallest details.

To improve the model we substituted custom-made pieces for some of the original elements; this was also more in keeping with its diminutive $\frac{1}{2}$ scale. We scratch-built the towing hook, the side handles, levers and steering wheel out of stretched plastic and

blue and brown tones using oil paints. When dry, we outlined all the details with a mix of black and brown.

This was all finished by applying a combination of Tamiya acrylic green enamels, combined with yellow (XF-4). The seat canvas was

copper wire. The dashboard clocks and the windscreen wiper were also custom-made from plastic rods and Roco-Minitanks glass. Other changes included the support for the spare tyre, the pedals and the holes on the rim.

(Vallejo 924) to lighten areas, especially towards the edges of the model. The white stripe and the stars were made using an airbrush and adhesive masks. Afterwards we added green,

then finished with beige green (Humbrol 90) and forest green (Humbrol 150), and the edges dry brushed. we finished by applying an overall coat of Marabú matt varnish.

Painting

The base colour is a mix of 60% dark green (XF-61), 15% Japanese green (XF-13) and 25% matt blue (XF-8). After airbrushing this mix, we used white (XF-2) and Russian uniform

The steering wheel and dashboard of a GAZ-67B in the Polytechnic Museum of Moscow (photo by Manuel Rodriguez Aguilar).

Bedford MW

Basic model-making is easy and fairly straightforward and will produce satisfactory results, but to make your models realistic requires an enormous amount of skill and patience. Certain techniques and skills need to be learned and practised but, when mastered, the entire model-making process — although hugely more challenging — becomes infinitely more rewarding.

Some of these advanced modelling processes are shown here with the emphasis on Allied vehicles operating in the North African desert.

Allied vehicles working in the desert during World War II require special treatment, — although, in fact, vehicles of both sides suffered an inordinate amount of erosion caused by the harsh desert weather conditions. Colour-wise the Allied vehicles differed little from the German vehicles — the former used a greenish bronze as the base to their 'sand' colour, whereas the Germans used a Panzer grey. The main difference was that many Allied vehicles, especially in the early stages of the war, sported colourful insignia.

This magnificent Bedford, built from scratch by Jorge Lopez Ferrer, will provide us with an example of a painting technique specific to wheeled vehicles possessing canvas and wooden parts.

Bedford MW

Building this model presents no technical problems at all, but the canvas awning is quite tricky. It is made out of modelling putty, pressed and then cut to shape. At this early stage it is important to put creases and pleats into the putty so that the successful rendering of the fabric is not only dependent on the paint job.

To show the dust clinging to the tire, airbrush a circle in the interior section.

Parts that have been chipped away by grit and rocks appear to suffer from the effect of rust and decay.

Wooden areas require a special 'damage' treatment to simulate peeling paint as well as wear and tear.

In some areas the chipping appears to reveal the original green base colour underneath.

The rest of the vehicle is made out of plastic with extra pieces from other models.

Keep in mind that this is a small lorry, much of it made out of wood and with no armour of any description. It therefore requires substantially different treatment from most military vehicles. A good paint job alone can make a small model like this look more spectacular than a large one, but to be successful, the work needs to be approached sensibly and reference material should be frequently consulted. Also bear in mind the areas where paint would have been chipped away and rust developed.

The bodywork of these lorries is much less robust than that of armoured vehicles and consequently they deteriorate

and rust quicker. The general effects, therefore, should be made with a light hand, with the washes being applied subtly, and the chipping virtually microscopic in size. Finally, a coat of dust covers the entire vehicle.

General Decoration

It is useful to know in which particular colours the truck would have been painted but, more importantly, the logical order of colour application and distribution over the vehicle should be understood before starting to paint the model. An understanding of this process will provide successful results regardless of the colours used. In this case we began by applying a very bright and saturated base colour; a colour approximating the original

without any bleaching (in other words, don't use white).

Subsequent layers in the places most exposed to the sun should be covered with lighter tones (colours less saturated and containing more white) and leave other areas with the original coat. This bleaching of certain parts of the surface should be worked progressively towards whiter tones and a matt finish. This approach will leave several areas possessing a glossy look, imitating the effects of the sun over the paint. A fine brown wash will unify the surface, but be careful to make it only a very light wash, so that the brightness and shine are retained where necessary.

Continue by outlining details in dark colours, and finish off by dry-brushing these areas to blend the painted elements in with the rest of the surface.

Approach the rendering of the eroded areas in two phases: first, simulate the rust in areas of metal surface only — focussing on damage around the mudguard and bumper; second, imitate the chipping away of paint and exposure of the underlying green base. This latter phase also includes imitating chipping and peeling paint on the wooden surfaces.

The canvas awning is the most complicated element to paint on this vehicle. In photos the canvas appears to possess a surprisingly wide variety of

After painting the whole tyre in black matt, put the dust in the centre with an airbrush, and to simulate the dust inside the grooves, grind a dust-coloured pastel crayon then apply the powder with a brush; afterwards, carefully brush off the remains with a soft, damp cloth. Cover the rest of the lorry in dust carefully and sensibly.

The canvas awning is covered with an extensive range of greys and greens to show the discolouring of age and use.

different colour tones, including patches made from different fabrics, areas that are damp, bleached, worn away, or simply dirty. The only common feature found on the surfaces of all desert vehicle awnings is the dust. In our case it will be important to emphasise the variety of tones, using a wide range of greens and greys. Drips imitating water or rain may be included. However, avoid using a dry brush because this makes the canvas appear to be made of stone or cardboard. To render highlights and worn-out areas, airbrush sandy colours in appropriate places.

Finally, the dust covering the various parts of the lorry is applied. On tyres, dust builds up in the centre with the rim area remaining relatively dust-free.

DODGE WC-56 3/4 TON

This model Dodge was the focal point of a large diorama featuring one of the many different vehicles used by General George Patton during the war. Due to the special role of his vehicles, they were supplemented with armoured bodywork in weak spots and equipped with .30 and .50 calibre machine guns. They were also equipped with powerful sirens, and panels containing emblems showing rank and group in order to provide easy identification.

This Italeri model at ⅓₅ is not very easy to find; the Italian manufacturer did not offer the Beep version of the WC-51 with the trunk (ref. 237), or the version equipped with a 37mm anti-tank canon (ref. 245). To transform the kit as accurately as possible, various pictures of the General's Dodge (now preserved in the Patton Museum of Kentucky) were used as reference. Further important document sources were generously supplied by Pedro Andrada, these provided a

The front plate is made of plastic and on its sides are a pair of adjustable pins. Note the fine chain wrapped around the capstan. (The chain comes from Verlinden).

Plastic sheet and copper wire were used to rebuild the interior of the vehicle.

The rear end of the vehicle was almost entirely rebuilt.

To get the characteristic shape of the horns we used plastic rods stretched under heat, afterwards, we cut and make them hollow.

The ammunition box — which also serves as a support for the machine gun — was made out of pieces of plastic.

The wings and footrest are built out of plastic. On the left side sits the spare tyre and a jerry can.

The various elements were made as follows: the seats were modelled with Milliput and then textured with surgical tape; the steering wheel was replaced by another made out of wire. The fuel pipe is custom-made and includes a heat-shaped plastic lid. The reflecting markers consist of resin copies of an original made out of plastic and wire, and on the tyres, (Verlinden) nuts were added as details. The flagstaffs and rod supporting the front view mirror are hypodermic needles inserted into entomology needles. The flags on the vehicle were designed on a computer then printed on a fine plastic sheet.

The bar separating the front and back seats is a copper cable, partially retaining the insulating coat. The bars of the roof are

great amount of specific detail for this particular vehicle.

The elements used from the kit were the chassis, wheels, capstan, bonnet, wings and bumper, headlights, windshield wiper, dashboard, tools, the driver, and the footrest. Other modifications were made using tin and plastic sheets, copper wire, stretched plastic, pieces of Evergreen, rivets, brass pieces, and various materials from a number of different sources.

The interior was remade using plastic sheets, with the side entrances outlined in wire. The rear wings were remade in accordance with the new bodywork, afterwards, the original footrest was sanded, outlined with wire and placed back in position. Located on the left side of the vehicle are the spare tire and a support for the jerry can. A compartment

for munitions and tools, which also serves as a support for a .50 calibre machine gun (by Tamiya decorated with wire and stretched plastic), is found over the footrest. The ammunition box and its support are built in accordance to the standard models used in US Army vehicles. Finally, an ammunition belt from another kit was added to this model.

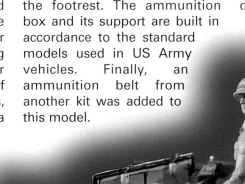

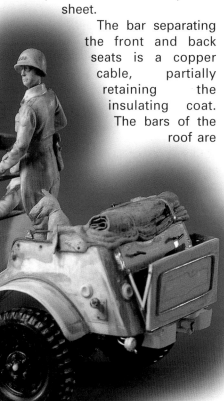

also made of this material while the convertible roof was made from Duro putty. The hooks for the roof canvas, and the bonnet mechanism are made of tin and rivets. The base of the antenna is made from a thin plastic sheet.

The front grille was replaced by one made of stretched plastic. Adjustable pins (identical to the ones used for the windshield wipers) were added on the sides of the plate covering the radiator. The window was made out of transparent acetate, on to which the rear-view mirror, windshield wipers, and wiring were added. The capstan was improved with the addition of plastic elements, wire, and Verlinden chain. The headlights include tin covers and the corresponding wiring. The horns were made out of stretched and hollow plastic, with tin supports obtained from a photo-engraving from Todo Modelismo.

The rear bumper and the protective plate are plastic sheets and strips of Evergreen — the pattern found on the plate is made out of wire. The drivers belong to the original Italeri model, but the jerry cans and much of the wiring were added later. After the painting stage, numbers and stars were applied to the surface. Depending on the surface, these elements were fixed by brush, adhesive masks, transfer sheets, or photo-engraved templates.

General Patton

One of the primary focal points of the diorama is the figure of General

The figure of General Patton was modelled out of putty using a Verlinden figure as reference and photos for his typical stance. Resin copies were then made of the original for future use.

Patton himself. The scene required a conspicuous, high quality and well-detailed figure able to command the centre of action. Unable to find a figure that met these requirements, we modelled General Patton out of Duro putty, using a Verlinden piece as reference. After examining several photos of Patton we tried to give the General his typical and habitual stance that he adopted during the European campaign. Once made, resin copies were taken for future use; as a matter of fact, the figure placed in the diorama is not the original.

The trousers, boots, shirt, tie, holster, medals and emblems were all modelled out of

versatile Duro putty. The head was also modified in order to form the General's famous features. On the front of the M1 type helmet, the five-point stars are made out of stretched plastic; the belts and pins, which were made out of a tin sheet and wire, were also added to the figure.

The General is shown wearing various rings which were made from slices of plastic which were then heated and reshaped. Afterwards, the rings were painted with a gold varnish, a colour which was also used to paint the jacket buttons and the belt buckle. The visible part of the revolver was carved out of plastic, and the trigger made from a fine wire; the butt was painted in a Vallejo ivory colour with the initials, 'G.P.' painted in red. The riding crop is made out of stretched plastic and tin, then painted acrylic brown.

The dog was also modelled using Duro putty, and copied in resin. The dog's colour scheme is a mix of white, pinkish dun and grey, with white added to lighten some areas.

The other figures

The reference for the other US military figures was obtained from Verlinden's US Tankers Warming Up (ref. 1105). By heating and reshaping, the same figure can be used for other figures throughout the scene and adapted to the different vehicles. The drivers arms were modelled in order to fit the steering wheels and handle bars, and the hands are from our stock collection. The heads and helmets are also Verlinden pieces. A touch of character can be added to faces with the addition of sun glasses, made out of copper wire. To complete the figures Colt gun covers were added (these were also part of our stock collection).

Harley-Davidson WLA

The motorcycles also belong to the old Italeri catalogue, and

COLOUR TABLE — Figures

Patton's army jacket, dark shirt, greenish brown trousers:
Base: American green (893) + olive brown (889) + carmine red (908)
Highlights: Base + brown ochre (856) + orange brown (981) + white (950)

Soldiers trousers, jackets, tie, leg warmers, light shirts:
Base: white (951) + brown ochre (856) + gold olive (857) + English uniform (921)
Highlights: Base + white (951)
Shading: Base + English uniform (921)

Olive green trousers, vehicle seats and canvas:
Base: Gold olive (857) + ochre brown (856) + black (950) + white (951)
Highlights: Base+ white (951) + brown ochre (856)
Shading: Base+ black (950)
(*To obtain a worn tone add white and yellowish brown to the base*)

Boots, wallets, gun covers and rifles:
Base: Chocolate brown (872) + black (950)
Highlights: Base+ brown ochre (856) + gold brown (877) + white (951)
Shading: Base+ black (950)
Finish: Satin varnish

Colour references from Vallejo Model Colour unless stated otherwise

include improvements and additions using the usual range of materials. The most outstanding improvements on the Harleys include the replacement of the original tire spokes for others made out of stretched plastic, the modelling of the leather wallets, and the new windscreen wiper made out of tin sheet and acetate.

Willys Jeep MB

This old Tamiya kit was improved with the same material as the other vehicles. The vast range of articles, photos and books about this vehicle helped to orientate the task. See also page 64. Additional details included the lowering of the suspension to indicate the weight of the

passengers. The roof was improved with putty, and the antenna and a variety of equipment were added. The girl's name was drawn then painted under the windscreen wiper.

Civilian vehicles

A civilian version of the Zundapp KS750 is found on the pavement. The reference for this motorcycle is rather old and had to be improved. Note the computer-generated license plates and the Zundapp emblems which are photo-engravings from The Show Modelling firm. To make the motorcycle appear more civilian, a bright acrylic coat of Tamiya black was applied.

Although it is not easily visible, a Mercedes automobile from an old Fujimi kit is found behind the large garage door. The bright black finish can be polished with Compound.

The entire diorama, was a slow and often exasperating job to perfect its many elements. It was awarded a silver medal in its category in a recent A.M.T. contest.

COLOUR TABLE Vehicles

Base: Olive green (Tamiya XF-62)
Washes: Burnt umber+ black (oil)
Dry brush, first coat: green (Humbrol 150)
Dry brush, second coat: green (Humbrol 150) + matt brown (Humbrol 26)
Dry brush, third coat: green (Humbrol 150) + matt brown (Humbrol 26)+ light brown (Humbrol 83)
Wear: Fine touches of black and silver
Dust/mud: Light brown (Humbrol 83) + matt white (Humbrol 34)

Jeep

**The word 'jeep' originates from the initials GP (General Purpose),
and refers to the small American, all-terrain vehicle extensively used
in all the fronts during World War II.**

The jeep is a remarkably robust vehicle, it is also agile and fast, with four motorised wheels which can cope with virtually any type of terrain.

With a 4-cylinder petrol engine, 2,199cc obtaining 54cv, three forward gears and one reverse gear, the jeep could carry 1,377kg of weight and drive up hills with 60% gradients, reaching maximum speeds of 105km/h.

As proof of its versatility the jeep was used as a command car, reconnaissance, ambulance, transport and anti-tank vehicle.

On occasion crawler tracks were experimentally mounted.

A staggering 640,000 jeeps had been manufactured by the end of the war. They were used across the world in places as diverse as Africa, Russia and the Pacific islands. Even in extreme environmental conditions the jeep was unfailingly reliable.

In the North African desert the jeep played an outstanding role in raids against Luftwaffe airfields. The jeep underwent considerable modifications with respect to the original design. All of the front grille bars except for two were cut off in order to facilitate cooling, and a

The rear end of the jeep is made out of etched steel.

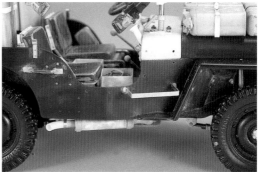

condenser, connected to the radiator by a tube, was adapted to recover evaporated water. The windshield was removed altogether and a solar compass device was installed, which marked the jeep's orientation by the shadow cast from a piano thread at the centre of a dial.

Several water and petrol containers were installed along with survival equipment, munitions, sleeping bags, etc.

The camouflage net, spare tires and devices used to get the vehicle out of sand banks were all considered indispensable.

These vehicles were heavily

The machine gun support is a section of thick hypodermic needle.

armed with three or five machine guns, 7.7mm Vickers, and some even carried a .50 calibre Browning rifle. Equipped with such fire power, the jeep could attack fuel depots and airfields at night, emerging from the desert like a ghost. When in a group, the vehicles adopted a V formation, firing outwards

A view of the underside of the jeep; the beige-coloured central protector is taken from the Tamiya SAS Jeep.

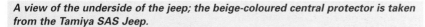

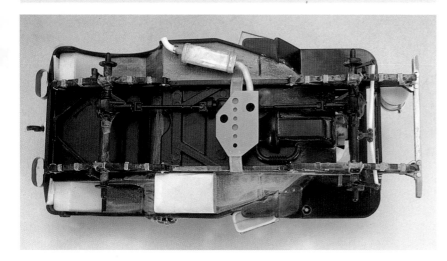

This canister was made using plastic and strips of tin.

The fitting of the hood was improved with a band of fine plastic.

from either side; as there was the danger of drivers getting hit by bullets, they had to remain seated in an upright posture to avoid fatal accidents.

After such a raid, the jeeps had to quickly retreat to the desert, dispersing and hiding under the camouflage nets before dawn to avoid being seen by enemy aircraft. Once out of danger, the vehicles regrouped and returned to the base

Jeep Assembly

Because the Tamiya SAS jeep leaves a lot to be desired we decided to use

the Italeri Commando jeep, and the excellent Show Modelling etched-brass kit.

We started by removing all but two of the bars protecting the radiator. Then, the many elements of the bodywork were glued on to the chassis. When making this model keep in mind that in the desert certain pieces such as the smaller lights, side and back handles were superfluous and as a result removed. Therefore, using a 0.20mm diameter drill bit we made the holes where the screws for such pieces would have been inserted. Six brackets on each side of the seat doorways were missing and had to be simulated using a 0.60mm drill. These brackets were used to hold canvases, which served as doors in cold and rainy areas.

Rivets were added to the sides. The bumpers and the rear side door were inserted — we used etched-brass which give a very realistic appearance.

Continuing on, we started adding detail to the lower end of the vehicle, including the clamps which join the various spring

The springs were painted with a Pactra rusty colour.

Detail of the machine gun and strapped canisters.

The chips on the surface of the jeep were rendered with rust colour tones , and the hose was painted in a brownish grey tone.

panels which can be imitated with strips of tin.

The anchor pieces between the chassis and springs were refined by gluing triangular sheets to each side; these triangular sheets are cut from etched-brass hexagonal hinges (after removing the relief). Copper wire was used to join the springs and axles.

After adding the rivets the exhaust silencer was rebuilt, and the tank was covered with a

A lot of detail was added to this dashboard with etched-brass bits from Show Modelling plus small plastic elements of copper wire, etc.

Note how the seats were painted in khaki tones and the rear section filled with all manner of equipment necessary for desert warfare..

fine plastic sheet to imitate a metal surface. After finishing this we moved on to the dashboard. This is an etched-brass piece to which the glove compartment door, support for the weapon butt, knobs, handles, etc, were added. The gear sticks were replaced by custom made metal ones.

The tube structure holding the seats was made out of telephone cable and plasticard was used to imitate the flaps which fixed the cushion and headrest to the model. Small cushions were also placed in the jeep to protect the drivers when operating through rough terrain.

When this was finished we returned to the bodywork. Our etched-brass kit only included one spare tyre support so we traced the metal over fine plasticard and carefully cut a second. Other details included gluing the small hooks for the canvas, rebuilding the side handles, making the canister out of plastic and making the machine gun tripods using

hypodermic needles. The front ends of the weapons were carefully hollowed out, and the carrying handles (made out of tin) attached to the munition drums.

The petrol cans are from Italeri (do not forget that the American ones have a chain attached to the lid). For this, plait

To paint the machine guns graphite was rubbed over a base of matt black enamel.

two fine metal wires to make the chain. The belts that support the cans are from the Todo Modelismo etched-brass kit no. 1 (SdKfz 232). The rest of the

The belts that hold the cans in place are from the Todo Modelismo etched-brass accessories kit.

elements come from different sources and some of them had to be made from custom made.

Painting the Jeep

We airbrushed a base mix of suede and desert yellow and lightened this with a softer spray of more diluted paint. For the shading we added earth tones, getting as wide a range of tones as possible that are different from the base colour. Paint the floor of the interior in an olive drab, concentrating the colour in the area where the driver and passenger rest their feet. To paint the surface of the seat, we airbrushed on khaki tones.

Using a dry brush, chipped paint was simulated in some areas with dark olive tones. The

In areas of friction and erosion, the British green appears through the sand colour. This effect appears in a more exaggerated way on the petrol cans.

canister and the platen holding the petrol were painted a rust tone.

After drying we applied overall washes using oil paints. To obtain chromatic diversity we carefully and gently washed with a mix of black, white, ochre, Naples yellow and burnt umber. Once dry, we outlined details to enhance the shapes with a mix that was slightly

Throughout the bodywork, green chip marks were combined with rust-coloured chips.

The cans with bluish-grey chipping are of German origin.

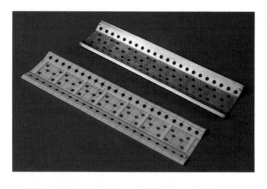

This device was made to get vehicles out of sand dunes. We built ours out of 0.2mm thick acetate and etched brass.

darker than the base colour. The edges were enhanced using a dry brush with light tones (carefully so as not to go over the chipping). Finally, we applied a coat of matt varnish.

Base and building

To build this small diorama we referred to travel magazines showing North African towns.

Once we had a clear idea of what we wanted we drew the ground plan and elevation, adapting the dimensions to the base. We took plasticard moulds of the facades using plaster and white glue. After drying, texture was added by using a metal bristled brush, a variety of files and a burin to engrave the stucco. The walls were glued and the joining areas were puttied.

A couple of coats of bright varnish were applied to harden the plaster surface and the ground was modelled with Das Pronto over the top of which a fine layer of sand was glued.

The building walls were made from 0.5mm plastic. The interior is a mix of plaster and white glue, tinted with ochre.

Painting the base and building

We modelled a dusty North African street corner with sun drenched buildings.

The mix used to colour the facades is a mix of a suede, medium grey and large quantity of white. For the ground surface, dark yellow, earth, suede and white were applied, combining the airbrush, wash, and dry brush techniques.

Figures

The two figures that appear in the foreground are Arab pieces and the heads of both were

After gluing the walls plaster was used to hide the joins. A coat of bright varnish was applied to harden the surface.

The back of the ruin was also made out of plaster and adapted to the circular shape of the base.

Fine sand is glued to the ground surface with white glue.

This small roof structure is made out of wooden rods, covered with bristles and a tin panel.

JEEP COLOUR TABLE
(*The airbrush colours are Tamiya acrylics*)

Airbrush:
Base: Desert yellow (XF-59) + suede (XF-57)
Highlights: Suede (XF-57)
Shading: Earth (XF-52)
Chips:
Chipping: Military green (975) + camouflage green (979) + matt earth (Vallejo 983)
Rusted chipping: Reddish brown (985) + black (Vallejo 950)
Transparencies:
Oils: White, yellow ochre, Naples yellow, burnt umber, black + white (grey)
Outlines:
Airbrush outline: Black (XF1) + matte brown (XF-10) + dark green (XF-61)
Brush outline: Naples yellow oil + yellow ochre + black + burnt umber
Brush:
Dry brush enamels: Khaki drill (72) + beige (103) + white + (34) (*all Humbrol*)
Varnish: Marabú Matte varnish
Weapon metals: Graphite over a black enamel base.

The bricks were carved with a burin and the rough texture of the surface was made with a brush with metallic bristles.

replaced by ones manufactured by Hornet; the beard and head piece of the figure wearing shorts was modelled with putty.

The soldier on the roof is a Hornet piece and its head was also replaced, in addition, the MP40 machine gun was placed beside him.

Interior view of the building. The lizard figure is included in a Dragon piece dedicated to the DAK.

BM-13 KATYUSHA

Following their first use in 1941, the Russian rocket launchers — known as 'Stalin's Organs' — became one of the best-known and feared weapons in the Soviet army's arsenal.

The model

It is a great shame to think that only Italeri has taken notice of these incredible pieces of equipment which were of great importance in the development of events during World War II. Fortunately, despite the age of

this Italian kit, (scale ⅟₃₅) it has stood the test of time and still remains an excellent model.

This Katyusha offers an enormous amount of detail from all angles, including the lower part, where the chassis, Cardan shaft and transmission are

accurately reproduced. This model (ref. no 242) is made up of over 100 pieces and is therefore ideal for model makers who particularly enjoy the assembly stage. For this reason (and because there are several tiny pieces) it is strongly

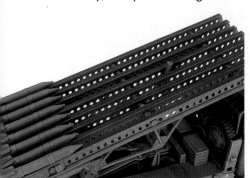

The rails and rockets were made made to look slightly dirtier by airbrushing with a matt black paint.

Tiny details, including dirt and erosion, were rendered with a brush, using matt black and a rusty brown.

The structure that supports the launch system allows for a slight elevation.

Assembly and painting

The first phase consists of assembling the lorry cabin, painting the interior with Russian Tank Green (Xtracolor X811) — the same tone will also be used for the exterior of the model. The seats can be black or brown leather; the latter was chosen here because it is more striking (Humbrol 180). The rest of the details, such as the dashboard, lever, etc, can be painted according to the

recommended that the manufacturer's instructions are closely followed.

After careful consideration we decided to assemble the model section by section, each of which would be also painted independently. If the model is built carefully, no problems should be encountered. The model has no flaws and being of fine quality plastic, is easily smoothed down and does not require the addition of much putty to join the seams.

The painting of these vehicles is not very spectacular, in fact it is monochromatic, nevertheless it requires the use of various techniques: airbrush,

Small elements can be added, such as detailing to the aiming mechanism.

dry brush and washes, in order to enhance an already highly detailed kit. For the reasons just mentioned, this article will focus on the painting phase.

instructions. The next stage will consist in the assembly of the various pieces that make up the chassis and transmission, painting the former with a base

To get tonal variations, several painting techniques will be combined over the vehicle's monochromatic colour scheme.

The radyal tires that come with the kit are made of rubber and should be repainted with matt black; afterwards, they can be aged with a sandy colour.

The high-quality reproduction of the head light covers and radiator grill from the kit make it unnecessary to replace these pieces by the often used etched-brass pieces.

COLOUR TABLE
Vehicle, launcher, and rockets: Green (Xtracolour X811)
Seats: Brown (Humbrol 180)
Chassis and transmission: Green (Xtractor X811), aluminum (Humbrol 56), and metallic grey (Humbrol 53)
Dirt and erosion: Sandy brown (Humbrol 63)

The model includes perfect copies of the protective metal sheets over the cabin.

colour of green (X811), and the axles with a metallic grey (Humbrol 53), and for small details, aluminium (56). This set of pieces may also be painted in satin black (Humbrol 85).

One of the most complicated stages involves the painting of the launching system itself, due to the difficulty in applying a dry brush to the many bars, rails and axles. The mobile parts should be put together carefully; but avoid gluing any parts that turn or revolve so they can still be elevated and turned.

The most laborious task is assembling and sanding the almost 50 pieces that form the M-13 rockets, which are also painted in green (Xtracolour X811). If desired, the vehicle could be painted as if it were part of a parade, in which case the choice could be made

between an aluminium or white colour.

Finally, the wheels are to be mounted, repainting the tyres in matt black (33), to eliminate the shiny quality of the rubber. The model does not include any special details, although it can be improved with the addition of small details, as we can see in the pictures.

The numbering on the vehicle consists of a simple number eight, painted in white, inside a square. This detail was seen in a photograph and obtained from a transfer.

To get a feeling of age and grime, the lower part of the lorry was softly airbrushed in sandy brown (Humbrol 63). The same can be done to the rails, but this time using black to more realistically show an operational Katyusha.

To age the lower section of the vehicle, softly shade off sandy brown (Humbrol 63) with an airbrush.

The vehicle number was painted over a transfer sheet.

The tube structure supporting the launching rails is one of the model's most fragile and delicate parts to mount.

ALBION AM463

This tanker lorry, used by the RAF, possessed a standardised chassis which the Scottish manufacturer Albion designed exclusively for the Air Defence Ministry in 1930.

Albion also used this same chassis to produce cranes and ambulances. All of these vehicles had a distance of 3.65m between axles and carried the same four-cylinder, 4,427cc engine with a four-speed gearbox and rear traction. The suspension was spring-based, although in some models the front suspension was replaced by a Guss type pneumatic system.

During the 1930s, some 1,900 of these vehicles were manufactured; they were also known as Albion 350 'petrol guzzler' because of the 1,325-litre (350gal) capacity of the tank. As well as the Albion, the six-wheel Morris Type Y1 was also used by the RAF during this period; it had a tank with a capacity of 2,280 litres (500gal), and the Karrier Type C had a capacity of over 13.6mt (15 tons).

Despite its cumbersome appearance, the Albion played an important role throughout World War II, and especially during the Battle of Britain, when it was a welcome sight for Hurricane and Spitfire mechanics. It was used on English airfields as well as abroad in the Near and Far East; after the war the vehicle remained in use. The Albion was in service for a total of almost 20

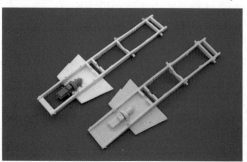

The base of the transmission and engine. Note the metallic rods that join together the chassis and interior floor.

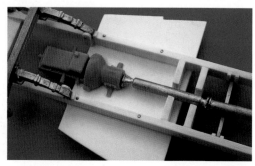

A view of the model after assembling the wheels

The rear axle is glued to the spring and reinforced with crossing metal rods.

years, but today it is a rare sight. The Albion was a light vehicle which was capable of simultaneously supplying three aircraft from its pumping unit which was adapted by Zwicky. This multi refuelling system was considered inefficient in times of war due to the movement of aircraft within the aerodrome.

A number of other tanker lorries saw action in Britain during World War II, one of the best known being the Bedford QL, an indestructible 4 x 4 which was in service up until the 1970s and which is still used in Scotland today.

The AEC854/Q854, was a monster of a vehicle, capable of carrying over 11,000 litres (2,906gal); a 6 x 6 version of the famous Matador used exclusively by Bomber Command for their aircraft and by Coastal Command for their Sunderlands.

The Thompson 3 x 2 is an interesting three-wheeler van with a front end fuel tank and room for the engine and driver in the rear.

Other vehicles that were used overseas included the Dodge T110, International K5, and variants of the CMP family (Ford and Chevrolet C60).

The Model

Made by Airfield Accessories in 1/35 scale, the model consists of a resin piece combined with white metal pieces. The quality of the kit is inconsistent, the best pieces are the tyres which completely lack flaws and are supremely well modelled.

However, air bubbles in the resin and a general lack of quality are found throughout the entire model, which in some cases is so bad that it is recommended parts be redone from scratch. Happily the shapes and proportions are accurate with the exception of a few small details which will be explained.

Assembly

Chassis

This piece is the first hurdle — as a piece of resin, with the motor block included, the chassis is curved and lacking in detail. After carefully thinking it over, we decided to discard this piece altogether without attempting to correct it by applying heat (past experience has shown that the piece eventually assumes the wrong shape).

Evergreen will help us in building this part of the model. Basing all our work on the original resin pieces we used the following references for the crossbeams:

The 179 (2.5 x 6.3cm), cutting two pieces to 14.9cm, these formed the main crossbeams and needed refining with a blade and file. We subsequently cut three pieces to 1.8cm which served as the central crossbeams.

The 177 (2.5 x 4mm) were also cut to 1.8cm; these served as the crossbeams for the rear end of the chassis.

Finally, the 178 (2.5 x 4.8mm) was cut to a length of 1.8cm and situated at the front end of the chassis.

All the joints of these pieces were reinforced with 0.5mm thick tin rods which were

The radiator was completely rebuilt; a great improvement on the original resin piece, seen right.

Roughs of the Albion logo were drawn out on the computer. The final version was a photo-engraving.

introduced prior to drilling. Finally, the base of the cab was made by superimposing two 1mm thick sheets of plasticard, each one previously cut in a trapezoidal shape. The engine was taken from the remains of another model, which in this case happened to be a British lorry.

The references for the following pieces are: tank supports (ref. 142 1 x 1mm), the buffers for the front end springs (ref. 142) and the tubes for the back end springs (ref. 223 tubes are 2.4mm). The nuts for these

tubes were also obtained from left-over bits of other models.

The central crossbeams needed to be brought down in size so as to place the transmission axle (made of white metal), as well as other elements, such as springs, front and rear end axles, exhaust pipe and tank supports. Reinforcing was necessary at the union of the rear axle and springs — achieved with a tin rod across the joint. The wheels were fixed to their respective axles by joining the two elements together using metal rods.

Radiator

This is another piece we entirely rebuilt. To create the radiator we used a 1mm thick sheet of plasticard, cut in the shape of the radiator base. Subsequently, we attached rectangular pieces along the edges (which were later sanded down to obtain the desired shape and inclination), hence creating a box, inside of which a fine metal fabric was placed. The front bars of the radiator were pieces cut to 1.5cm long (ref. Evergreen 100/0.25 x 0.5mm). For other details various flat surfaces were

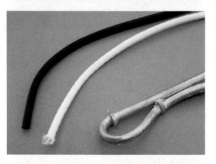

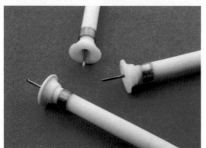

The fuel funnels were copied in resin.

A view of the funnels attached to the tubes. The hose clips are made of metal.

Electric cable or rubberised cloth can be used to make the hoses.

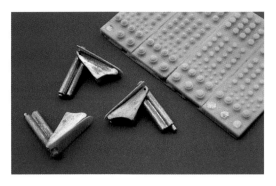

The supporting pieces, tube and hose prepared for painting.

The new supports for the bumper, made from plastic and tin sheet.

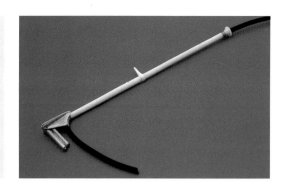

used, and a leather punch was used to create the lid on the radiator. The Albion nameplate label was made by Eduardo Soler, firstly with a rough draft on the computer then finally as a photo-engraving with the usual chemical processes.

Hosepipes

The funnel ends of the hosepipes were made out of resin, based on an original created by Ramón Domingo using a block of plastic, a small drill and a blade. The original kit pieces were made out of white metal and modelled as whole pieces together with their tube, but these pieces were small and unconvincing when compared against period photographs. Once the funnels were glued to the hosepipes, hoseclips made out of aluminium sheet, were added. The central turnbuckle supports of the tube were made

The tube supports were improved with Verlinden screws and plastic

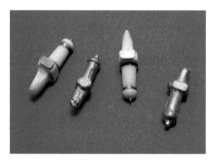

The support and the spare hose were also made from Contrail and Evergreen material.

View of the placement of the bumper supports.

The inside of the cab after painting. The seat has a leather finish and the wood is showing through the most worn areas of the floor.

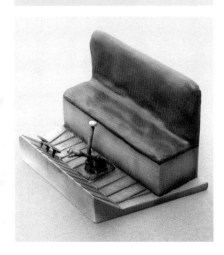

using Evergreen 104 (0.25 x 2mm) in a delicate operation that required careful filing (due to the fragility of the piece) of the upper part of the support. To make the actual hosepipes we could do one of two things: use 2.5mm thick electric cable, or covered rubber bands (the sort found in post offices) which are more flexible; we decided to use the latter.

The tube supports are the white metal originals but improved with 0.5mm plasticard and Verlinden's largest screws.

The spare hose was made from scratch, with the support being made by referring to Evergreen (ref. 263 2mm U-profile, and ref. 104 0.25 x 2mm strip). The hose is a Contrail tube with a tin rod through the middle — this allows both the hose and support to be bent.

Fender supports

These were also rebuilt using several round and square Evergreen surfaces, tin sheet, brass rods and Reheat (RH035 at 1/32) for the fender sheets.

Cab

In this case the original was used, but with the following improvements: the seat was remodelled with Squadron putty because the originals had an exaggerated shape; the pedals (Evergreen) were added, and the levers and brakes were brought in from another model.

The seats were painted with Decorfin acrylics (ref. 402, 411 and 422), giving it a leather finish. The rest were painted in the same colour as used for the exterior but making worn down areas to reveal the original wooden surface (with Vallejo acrylics light and gold brown, and a number 1 or 0 brush). We outlined the gaps between the wooden deck boards with a diluted raw umber oil colour.

The instrument panel was improved by adding Reheat rings (RH023 at 1/32), and the

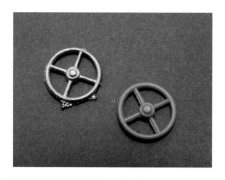

The steering wheel was replaced by a similar one taken from a collection of unused pieces.

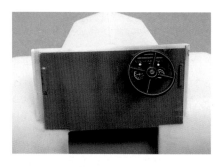

A view of the dashboard, with the steering wheel in place.

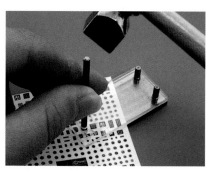

The dials on the instrument panel are a Reheat product, and were cut with a leather punch.

steering wheel was replaced. The dials from the instrument panel were obtained from Reheat (RH09 at 1/48) using a leather punch.

A wooden structure made by Evergreen (157-1.5 x 4mm) was placed on the headrest of the seat.

Bonnet and cab exterior

In both cases the original resin pieces were used, but new improvements were made.

The original central bonnet rod was substituted by an Evergreen (ref. 219 0.64mm) rod. The flaws of the cab were corrected, a lock was added (Reheat RH023 1/32) as well as a handle (tin rod), the hinges (0.6mm hypodermic needles), and other small details using Evergreen and Reheat.

Fuel supply control panel

Here we also used the original but made our own changes. This

The hinges were made from parts of hypodermic needles. There are also Reheat and tin rod details.

Putty was used to cover the flaws around the inside of the cab. The interior wooden structure was made with plastic rods.

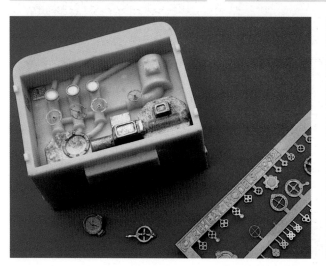

The rear doors were rebuilt using plastic sheets; locks and bolts were also added.

Reheat Models etched-brass pieces replaced the original white metal.

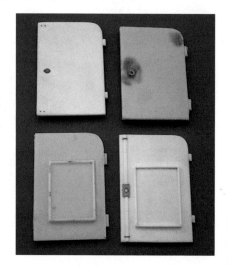

The ladders are made by Plastruct. The edges were rounded with a file and the piece was curved in hot water.

The resin footrests were replaced with ones made of plastic.

part of the vehicle is essentially made up of two pieces: the resin box where the various tubes are found and the fuel extraction tank made out of white metal. The three pressure gauges were newly created using Evergreen pieces and Reheat photo-engravings. The valve taps were also substituted by photo-engravings (Reheat RH046 at 1/48). Finally, the sheets and aeration panels were added.

To complete this section, we added the pressure gauge dials (Reheat or Waldron), some notices and other Waldron accessories.

The inside was painted in white, while the tubes were airbrushed in Model Master metallic colours. The effects of aging were done following the usual painting processes. However we had to keep in mind that the colours will

The spare tire requires a support so it can be placed on the right side.

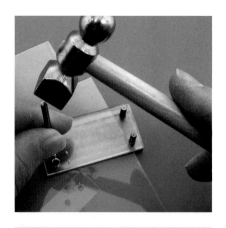

Use a leather punch and an acetate sheet to make the glass for the headlight.

change and that Model Master paints are not compatible with enamels and oils; therefore, our treatment had to be acrylic and water based. The inside of the doors have Verlinden data panels.

The rear doors
The doors were built from scratch using 1mm thick plastic sheet and adding locks, bolts, hinges and data panels.

The tanker
This piece is well formed but had numerous surface bubbles which required a lot of work. The tank itself should be about 3mm longer to be correctly in scale. We solved this problem by attaching two 1.5mm plasticard sheets to each end.

Noticed the aged look on this side view of the cab.

A strip of Evergreen (0.25 x 0.50mm) was added to the base of the petrol cap.

Other accessories
Ladder
We discarded the original kit ladders and replaced them with Plastruct stairs; the new ladders required retouching to make the square-shaped bars round. To do this we filed the bars down then put the ladders in hot water in order to curve them (this must be done very carefully as the pieces are easily damaged). The ladders were attached to

Here we can see the tubes and hose supports, including the spare piece.

two Evergreen rods which were drilled into the tanker.

The running boards
These pieces were remade in order to show the wood grain so it could be emphasised in the painting stage.

Fuel tank
The original is magnificent, and therefore does not need to be changed.

Headlights
These pieces were taken from the remains of other kits. Transparent plastic (stretched under heat) was used to make the bulbs that were inserted into

the large headlights (these lights did not have protective glass).

The same approach was used with the bulbs for the smaller lights, the glass on these lights were made by using transparent acetate and a leather punch.

Spare tyre
The original support was removed and a new one was made using Evergreen material to make fixing easier.

License plates
The kit did not provide this detail and after referring to period photographs, we wrote the plates on a computer, then printed them with an ink jet printer onto a glossy paper — this helped to achieve the desired effect of maximum quality and material consistency.

Starting handle
Because the original white metal piece is flawed we created a new one using a tin rod and a hypodermic needle.

RAF inscription
This is a Decadry transfer.

Hose supports
We based our work on photographic reference and we should mention that there were a variety of shapes. We used Evergreen pieces.

The rear section of the vehicle, now painted and with the dials, panels and other elements in place. The data panels found on the inside of the doors are from Verlinden.

phases, covering all required areas of the model at each phase before moving on to the next painting phase (for example, if we were in phases 6, 7, 8 'transparencies', we would paint each area throughout the whole vehicle before moving on to the following phase).

This way of painting the model is a step-by-step approach, but it is not the only method that may be used. In the end, what matters is the result. For example, there are those who like to apply phase 4 'aging' after phases 8 or 9. If the proper order is followed however, there will be a greater

Other elements

The windscreen was made from an acetate sheet and a photo-engraving of a windscreen wiper was also added. The rearview mirror was made entirely from plasticard and a tin rod. The bumper was an Evergreen rod, with reference 222 (a section of 1.6mm). The cables of the hosepipe turnbuckles were made from stretched plastic.

Painting

The Albion varied in colour depending on the time period and theatre of operations. The commonest colour was dark earth, but it was not unusual to see the vehicle painted in the colour used by British fighters during the Battle of Britain (green + dark earth).

After analysing several photographs we decided not to use the simple colour scheme of dark earth. Instead we based our colour selection on the Federal Standard 595a and its colour reference 30118. For those who do not have the F.S. available, Humbrol colour number 29 will work as well.

The entire lorry was painted in the same way as the rear door. We worked in demarcated areas, through successive

The right side ladder, in place and painted, and surrounded by areas of greater wear and tear than on other parts of the lorry.

absorption of the paint, and the results will be more subtle. Therefore, the final look needs to be considered when painting the model.

The lower sections of the vehicle were covered with Tamiya XF-10, applied with an airbrush, and focusing in the areas where mud build-up was simulated (with putty and sand).

Drips from minor fuel leaks and spills on the top of the tanker were made using black oil paint.

The hoses were covered in black and afterwards gradually painted in greys and neutral colours with a dry brush. The texture of the elastic (rubber bands) will make the rendering of volume relatively easy.

DODGE WC-54

This small vehicle is a classic model from the catalogue of the Italian manufacturer Italeri (scale ⅟₃₅). Here we are showing the straightforward construction of the model as described with the kit. This vehicle requires very few improvements.

We started with the assembly of the chassis, which is put together by following the instructions included in the kit. This assembly phase requires careful work, especially when it comes to the levelling and alignment of the wheels, in order to avoid the model ending up unbalanced. Also take particular care when fitting the lower bars and differential — if they are forced they will appear to be sagging and consequently look unrealistic.

The interior

This Italeri model includes two pieces for the interior, one of which is not readily visible from the outside, and the other which can be easily seen from the rear side of the vehicle. This makes our job easier, for we can prepare the inside pieces by refining them with Scotch Brite. The interior is worked on by adding the clutch pedal and brakes, all made from small pieces of plastic with horizontal lines scratched across the surface. These pieces are fixed into position by gluing them to a wire with cyanoacrylate. The front seats, the front doors, steering wheel, handbreak, etc., are all placed after the interior has been painted.

Once this is all prepared, we filled the airbrush with white matt acrylic (Tamiya XF-2) and layered

the interior with two or three fine coats of paint until the dark green colour of the plastic was completely covered. After cleaning the airbrush, we filled it with a very diluted acrylic brown red (XF-64), and shaded every corner of the interior, the rivets of the rear box, etc. Shading is then airbrushed into place — most is sprayed onto the ground, less on the sides and very little on the ceiling. When working on the rear side doors, decrease the intensity as you progress upwards. When painting the closing mechanism, pay most attention to the bars.

The next job are the seats and the details that need to be added to the front doors — this is all done using a grass green enamel (Humbrol H-80). Using Humbrol colours we also painted the lights, gauges, handles, clutch, etc. Once this work was finished, we left it to dry completely for three days. Then we applied light oil washes using a burnt umber diluted in Titan turpentine, covering every corner of every piece. Afterwards we used the dry-brush technique to highlight all the edges and rivets. The green areas, seats and doors were also worked with a dry brush, making the grass green lighter with white matt (H-34). The steering wheel and lever can be made slightly lighter by adding a touch of dark grey.

The last job was to render the chipped surface material with black and silver enamel. We reduced the contrast of the silver by applying a light, dry coat of sand (Humbrol H-63) and dark earth (H-29), which is also used on the floor and lower door.

Once the paint in the interior was dry, we carefully placed the transparencies in position using white glue; we closely followed the kit instructions so as to apply the glue with precision. the model was left to dry thoroughly before continuing.

The exterior bodywork

We strongly recommend that you do not glue the radiator and front bumper until right at the very end, as it is almost impossible to paint the inside of the headlights and radiator without making a mess. The radiator is painted matt black followed by a light dry-brushed coat of gun metal.

On the outside the only improvements consist of replacing the support for the rearview mirror for one made of fine wire and the addition of the front and back door handles made out of stretched plastic. The remainder were made according to the assembly instructions.

At this stage we added a little ordinary putty to the underside of the vehicle to simulate the

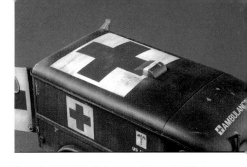

inevitable build-up of mud. This was stipple textured with a thick bristle brush.

To provide the vehicle with a greater sense of weight, we sanded down the sides of the wheels where they touch the ground. To be able to paint all around the wheels we supported them on small, thin sticks. The doors, which will remain open, were attached by applying a touch of white glue to ensure that they remain fixed during the painting process and the interior does not get covered in green. We used maskol and adhesive tape to mask out the transparencies.

Exterior painting

We decided on an olive drab colour scheme, typical of the U.S. Army of the period. We began by applying an airbrushed base made up of 70% olive drab (XF-62) and 30% dark green (XF-61). To lighten this combination we added dark yellow (XF-60) and buff (XF-57). At this stage we particularly concentrated on the

roof and accentuated its rounded edges, which if carefully coloured and lightened will look very elegant. The same treatment was then applied to the front bumper and bonnet. When all this was safely dry we fixed the wheels into place; the rubber areas needed to be painted black and lightened with a touch of ochre.

The next stage consists of adding the numerals and insignia. In the case of this model such elements were either traced, dry transferred or painted using masks. The series numbers and unit identifications are part of the kit tracing sheet. To get the final placement perfect, it is important to apply a coat of bright varnish on the spot where the insignia will be transferred. Place the symbol using Micro liquids and apply a final coat of matt varnish, preferably using an airbrush.

The transfers consist of stars and the word 'Ambulance', both of which come from Verlinden. The two red cross

symbols on the sides are cut-out tracings and applied as before. At this stage it is important to airbrush over a coat of matt varnish to prevent the transfers from getting damaged during subsequent washes.

After unsuccessfully trying to trace the large red crosses, we decided to paint them using masks and an airbrush. The masks were made using tape and transparent adhesive tape. These masks are very easy to make. The only difficulty lies in flattening the top mask against the curved surface of the roof, which we solved by applying Maskol to prevent any paint from escaping under the mask and staining the olive drab. Nevertheless, if any paint does escape, go over the relevant area with very diluted paint. The US Army Medical Corps symbol was done with a brush (you can use a transfer).

Again the model was left to dry for at least three days. On resuming, we applied a number of overall oil paint washes, making strokes on the surface of the ceiling and armoured areas with ochre, cream and white paint. A wash was then applied to all the corners and onto specific areas such as the fender and into any dirty brown cracks in order to enhance the sense of depth.

Once dry, carefully lighten the edges with a dry brush with a mix of enamel white, yellow and green (Humbrol H-34, H-94 and H-155). Render surface chipping with silver and a bit of green and matt dark earth, matt sand and matt khaki drill (Humbrol H-29, H-63 and H-72) on the tyres and the lower ends of the vehicle. Subsequently apply a light coat with a dry brush to render the effects of dust and dirt.

To make the dust along the lower edges we used a diluted matt dark earth, sprayed on with an airbrush from a distance of approximately 25cm. We also sprinkled drips of paint in this area, to give a realistic sense of use and travel. At this stage we focussed on the working areas such as the lower end of the front bumper and the lower edges of the tires to provide stronger visual impact. Everything was left to dry for a few days then finished with a coat of matt varnish to the entire vehicle to unify the surface texture and eliminate any unwanted shiny surfaces.

To fill the inside of the Dodge ambulance we added a canvas made from glued tissue paper, a backpack and a Verlinden box of food.

VW-86 KÜBELWAGEN

Conceived during the early stages of World War II, the versatile and popular Kübel soon became known as one of the finest vehicles of the war

Assembly and details

This model is excellent, a fine design with perfect fittings and fun to assemble; however, considering the expensive price tag, the manufacturer should have considered the problem with the folding of the convertible roof (reference HB1 and HB2) which we had to model with putty.

We are going to use an Eduard etched-brass sheet (ref. 35024). Remember, however, that etched brass is not the solution for everything; as flat material it often shows details as having a lack of, or an excess of, volume (as is the case here with the vehicle pedals), so only use etched-brass kits and accessories in appropriate situations where they enhance rather than detractor or distort the model.

We started with the interior, adding the fuel dials and parts of the fuel tank which need fine plastic tubes and the remaining pieces of etched brass. Newly built elements included the handbreak, the starter, light switch and sheet holders on the insides of the doors, for which plastic, acetate, phone cable, and other materials were used.

A diagram showing the placement of these elements is shown on page 61. Pieces of Evergreen were used to make the bar structure on the front seats. Before fitting the various parts of the body together we airbrushed the pieces — in the process covering the areas that will be inaccessible once joined.

In the lower parts of the

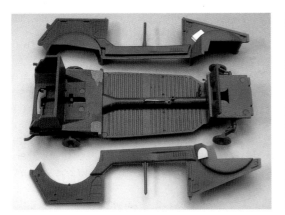

A general view of the pieces added to the interior.

A view of the finished seat.

With the edge of a blade, the transmission protector was refined.

The building of the frame of the convertible roof.

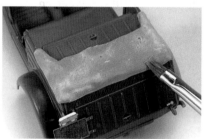

The first coat of putty being smoothed out with a flat brush.

Marking and placement of the tire valves.

To make the folds, we used various precision modelling tools.

vehicle the protective sheet of the transmission was refined, the exhaust pipes were hollowed, and the tyre valves were added using stretched plastic.

On the exterior, etched brass was used for the back lights, license plates, door handles, etc. Using a very fine material

add cables to the small lights. On the sides of the small engine doors, two loops, (made of plastic rivets and etched brass) were placed.

Drill small holes on the top edges of all four doors to fit the detachable windows.

The small chain attached to the tank lid was made using copper wire. The subtle effects of denting on the mudguard were made by putting a lit cigarette next to the surface.

The convertible roof was modelled using a putty made up of two components which were applied in successive layers one over the other. On the last layer we placed a piece made out of plasticard and putty. The bars were built out of extra pieces of etched-brass sheets, and fine

plastic tubes as illustrated in the diagram.

The canvas is supported by five belts on the back side, and three on the two lateral sides. We made these belts starting from a strip of tin, cut into 2.5mm long pieces.

Finish off the roof by adding an appropriately cut and sized piece of plastic.

A view of the finished convertible roof.

Etched-brass belt supporting hooks.

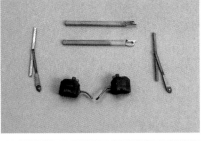

The elements that form the windshield.

We began by airbrushing a base colour mix of dark yellow, suede and cinnamon. This mix was altered to get lighter and darker versions.

To create the camouflage a mix of olive green, JA green, khaki and dark yellow were used; vegetation-like shapes were drawn out as part of the camouflage pattern.

A high performance airbrush and strong compressor are not enough to render camouflage. It is important to remember to first spray on paper and continue adding to the paint supply. The air pressure is crucial, with ½kg being the optimum. After finishing the camouflage, the seats were painted black, with earth colour highlights.

The usual washes were applied using oil paints. Outlining was done with a mix of burnt umber and yellow ochre; the mix was lightened with a dry brush using enamels lighter than the base colour. Chips and rust were next; the bonnet was painted field grey and after adding an earthy tone to the lower end of the vehicle it was finished with a matt varnish.

The Notek headlight was replaced by a G Sangyo headlight.

The placement of etched-brass pieces on the rear of the vehicle.

General view of the interior.

Some rivets were added over the shovel

A detail of the rods of the convertible roof.

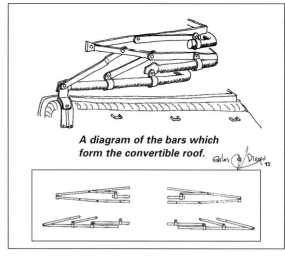

A diagram of the bars which form the convertible roof.

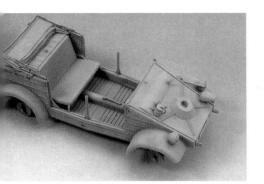

The base colour, from which various shades were created.

A typical camouflage pattern used in areas of dense vegetation.

A view of the small hooks which fix the windscreen wiper in a lowered position.

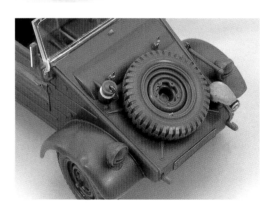

1. Starter
2. Light switch
3. Fuel indicator
4. Sheet holder
5. windshield wiper motor
6. Roof hooks

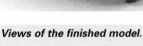

Views of the finished model.

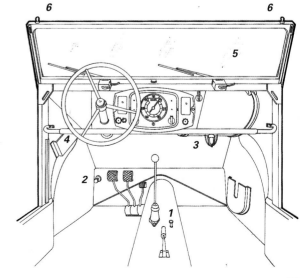

The application of an adhesive mask while painting the seats

COLOUR TABLE
(sand and green colour scheme)

Tamiya acrylics
Black (XF-1)
Khaki (XF-4)
JA green (XF-13)
Matt earth (XF-52)
Cinnamon (XF-55)
Suede (XF-57)
Olive green (XF-58)
Dark yellow (XF-60)

Vallejo acrylics
German uniform (920)
Grey olive (a-94)
Black (a-95)

Humbrol Enamels
White (34)
Oak (71)

Titan oils
White (4)
Burnt umber (78)
Yellow ochre (88)
Transparent gold ochre (94)

Marabú varnish
Mattlack

The seat painted and in position.

The dents on the mudguard were made by applying heat. With a fine brush, render the effects of chipping and apply touches of a rust colour.

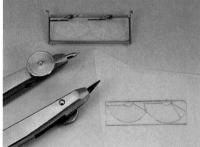

A drawing of the mask used to make the dust effect on the windscreen

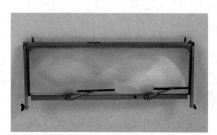

The result is quite good.

A detail of the convertible roof, with the hooks, belts, and bars in place.

Adhesive masks were also used to paint the license plates.

A view of the back seats and dashboard after completion.

The numbers on the license plates are transfers. The division emblem was hand painted.

The front end axle was placed with the wheels slightly turned.

The effects of dry brush over the edges of the model; combining this technique with washes and outlining provides a very realistic sense of volume.

The black base colour of the seats was lightened by air-brushing over a brown tone.

WILLYS JEEP

The Willys Jeep at ⅟₄₈ scale is an excellent component to add to an aviation diorama.

the Willys Jeep is readily available in many publications. To add the emblems, use the 'WWII US Army Type Stars' Verlinden transfer sheet.

The paint job was began by airbrushing the entire vehicle with a coat of Olive drab (Tamiya XF-62). Afterwards, the jeep was aged by applying various green

The side handles were made using copper wire.

This Verlinden model (ref. No. 522) of the legendary American jeep is, generally speaking, authentically correct. Because the kit is modelled out of polyurethane resin and photo-engraved metal pieces, the

assembly is easy and quick; however, the cleaning of the finer pieces needs to be done very carefully and cautiously due to the fragility of the material. All of the pieces found in this model were joined using cyanoacrylate glue, with the exception of the plastic windscreen, which will be inserted between the metal frames using white glue. It is worth noting that the handbrake and gearlever pieces were made separately out of stretched plastic and the lateral handles were made using copper wire.

Despite its small size, the Willys Jeep can include detail found on a much larger scale model. Reference material for

By applying green and ochre tones with a dry brush, the model acquires a lively quality.

and ochre tones using a dry brush technique. The lightest tones and brightest colours were used on the seats, headlights and instruments. The kit also includes a radio unit which can be assembled into the model if desired.

The insignia on the bonnet is an adhesive transfer from Verlinden found on sheet 159.

The handbreak and gear lever were made from stretched plastic.